CONTENTS

ONLINE ACTIVITIES

On some of the pages you will see QR codes. These QR codes take you to online Purple Mash activities which support learning from the relevant page.

To use the QR codes, scan the QR code with the camera on your web enabled tablet, click on the link and the activity will appear on screen.

Alternatively, QR readers are available on the app store for your device.

SCAN CODE

purple mash

Published 2024. Little Brother Books Ltd, Ground Floor, 23 Southernhay East, Exeter, Devon EX1 1QL
books@littlebrotherbooks.co.uk | www.littlebrotherbooks.co.uk
Printed in the United Kingdom
The Little Brother Books trademark, email and website addresses, are the sole and exclusive properties of Little Brother Books Limited.

LB BOOKS

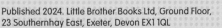

NOUNS

Charlie Brown is known by many names, including Charles and Chuck.

The word for the names of things are **nouns**. A **noun** is a naming word for things, places, people, or animals. There are two main types of **nouns**:

Proper Nouns	Common Nouns
Charlie Snoopy Linus A **proper noun** is the name for a particular person or place, e.g., Woodstock and America. Proper nouns must always start with a capital letter.	girl bird school A **noun** (or **common noun**) is the more general name for people, things, places or animals, e.g., boy, cat, book.

1

Can you help Charlie sort these **nouns** into person, place, animal and thing?

pond room chair squirrel boy plane friend cookie bike library sister town teacher rabbit

person	place	animal	thing

2

Dog is the **noun** for any dog. Snoopy is the name of a particular dog so it is a **proper noun** and starts with a capital letter.

Circle all the **proper nouns**.

Lucy   cupcake   day   Sally   brother
Tuesday   fruit   fun   fair

FINGER SPACES

Charlie is the manager of the Peanuts gang's baseball team. Charlie is reading a book about baseball to try and help the team improve and he's noticed there are spaces between words.

1

As you read each sentence, touch the baseballs to add finger spaces between the words. Then count the number of words in each sentence.

a. Baseball ⚾ is ⚾ a ⚾ great ⚾ sport.　　　　= _____ words

b. Players ⚾ must ⚾ work ⚾ as ⚾ a ⚾ team.　　= _____ words

c. Teams ⚾ should ⚾ practise ⚾ lots ⚾ to ⚾ improve.　= _____ words

2

Copy each sentence from question 1, leaving a baseball sized space between each word. The first one has been done for you.

> Remember: Capital letters and full stops.

a. Baseball　is　a　great　sport. _____

b. _____

c. _____

3

One of the headings in the book is hard to read because it's been written without **finger spaces**. Can you work out what it should say? Write it underneath with the spaces.

Learnhowtowinatbaseball

_____

3

HANDWRITING

Peppermint Patty doesn't write very neatly! Miss Othmar couldn't read her latest book report so she's asked Peppermint Patty to practise her handwriting. Can you join her and practise yours too?

1

This group of letters are long ladder letters.

i   j   l   t   u

Can you write each letter 5 times? Start at the top, go straight down, then finish the letter.

i

j

l

t

u

2

Copy these words three times with a space between each word. Sound them out as you write

it _____ _____ _____

jilt _____ _____ _____

tut _____ _____ _____

SENTENCE BUILDER —✶

As you know, Snoopy doesn't speak but Charlie Brown can understand him perfectly. Charlie knows how sentences are made and that every sentence he says to Snoopy will have a **noun** and a **verb**.

The **phone is ringing**.

Noun
Who or what the sentence is about.

Verb
Tells us what the noun is doing.

1

Choose a word from each box below to make a sentence that describes each picture. The first one has been done for you.

Who (Noun or Pronoun)
Charlie
Snoopy
(Pig Pen)
Linus

Doing what (Verb)
is driving
(is walking)
is smiling
is falling

a. Pig Pen is walking. _____

b. _____

c. _____

d. _____

Read your sentences. Do they make sense? Did you remember to put a capital letter at the beginning and a full stop at the end?

Remember: Capital letters and full stops.

2

Snoopy has been writing with his typewriter but it's got jammed and the words have been mixed up! Can you rearrange them so that each sentence makes sense?

a. busy the library is _____

b. is day hot it a _____

c. Charlie talking is _____

5

ee SOUND

Sally loves playing on the s**ee**-saw at the park. See-saw has a long **ee** sound. The words below all have the same sound but there are different ways of spelling that sound.

1 Help Sally sort the words below by writing them in the correct boxes.

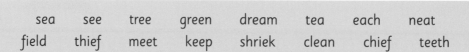

| sea | see | tree | green | dream | tea | each | neat |
| field | thief | meet | keep | shriek | clean | chief | teeth |

ee	ea	ie

Can you think of more words with the long **ee** sound?

2 Choose the correct word from the table above to fill in the gap in each sentence, then write the remaining letters.

a. Linus always remembers to clean his t_____ before bed.

b. Sally likes visiting the beach and swimming in the s_____.

c. Peppermint Patty wears a gr_____ shirt.

d. Charlie's kite often gets stuck in a tr_____.

e. Marcie keeps her bedroom n_____ and tidy.

f. Snoopy likes to run in the f_____.

6

COMPREHENSION

Sally is off to summer camp. She's been given a brochure telling her all about it.

The camp is in the middle of nowhere and it's so dark at night you can't even see your own feet! There are lots of trees to climb and you sleep in cabins made of wood. There's a lake where you can go swimming and on the last day there's always a river-raft race. There's a tuck shop where you can buy snacks.

1 Put a tick to show if each sentence is true or false.

	True	False
a. The camp is in a city.		
b. There are lots of trees.		
c. You cannot swim in the lake.		
d. The cabins are made of wood.		
e. You can buy snacks at the supermarket.		

2 Draw a picture of what you think the summer camp might look like.

PLURALS

Charlie is always trying to fly a kite. He's owned many kites but they always end up broken after crashing to the ground or getting caught in the kite-eating tree!

We use the plural of a word to show more than one of that thing.
Adding an **s** is the most common way to make most singular words plural, but some words need **es**.

kite = one kite   kites = lots of kite**s** (plural)

Sally has bought Charlie a new kite and has wrapped it up in a box. Because box ends in an **x**, to make it plural you must add **es**.

box = one box   box**es** = lots of box**es**

If you say the word out loud, you can sometimes hear if it needs **s** or **es**.

Words that end in **s** always need **es** to make them plural.

Words that end in **sh**, **ch** and **x** also need **es** to make them plural.

1

To make most words plural, you add an **s** at the end.

Change these words to make more than one by adding **s**.

a. snail _____   **b.** door _____   **c.** egg _____   **d.** home _____

But some words need **es** adding at the end to make them plural. Change these words to make more than one by adding **es**.

e. brush _____   **f.** church _____   **g.** fox _____   **h.** lunch _____

2

Have a go at adding **s** or **es** to these words. Say them out loud and check the ending to help you choose.

a. one burger   lots of _____   **d.** one kiss   lots of _____

b. one wish   lots of _____   **e.** one beach   lots of _____

c. one ball   lots of _____   **f.** one dish   lots of _____

VERBS

Miss Othmar is teaching the class about **verbs**. There's lots to learn so Charlie and his friends will need to concentrate!

Did you know?
Verbs can be past, present or future tense.

Did you know?
There are different types of **verbs**.
Action verbs are easiest to recognise e.g. walk, talk, think.

Did you know?
Every sentence must have a **verb** in it.

Did you know?
A **verb** tells us what someone or something is doing and sometimes feeling.

Marcie **wears** glasses.

Peppermint Patty **yelled**.

Woodstock **is** laughing.

Snoopy **feels** tired.

1

Here are some **action verbs**. Can you mime an action for each one?

a. swim   **b.** sing   **c.** shrink   **d.** exercise   **e.** climb

f. Can you think of two more action verbs? _____ , _____ .

2

Underline the **action verb** in these sentences. Look for the words saying what the characters are doing, or what is happening. **Verbs** can also be things that have already been done.

a. Peppermint Patty is skating.

b. Charlie was waiting patiently for Snoopy.

c. Sally ate a cupcake for pudding.

d. Playing baseball is fun.

3

Think of your own **verb** to put in each sentence.

a. Charlie is _____

b. Snoopy _____ every day.

c. Linus was _____ yesterday.

Remember to read the sentence to check it makes sense.

STORY SEQUENCING

It's a snow day and school is closed – hurray! Charlie is building a snowperson. He follows a sequence to make sure he builds it in the correct order.

1 Number each sequence to put the steps needed to build a snowperson in the correct order.

Decorate the snowperson.

Roll a smaller ball of snow for the head.

Roll a large ball of snow for the body.

Place the head on top of the body.

2 Franklin has joined Charlie so they can go sledging in a cardboard box. Can you work out the order they need to do the things below? The first one has been done for you.

First,   they sit in the box.

Then,   they drag the box to the top of the hill.

Next,   they slide down the hill.

Finally,   they push off from the top of the hill.

Pretend to be Charlie and act out the four steps above. Be quick though, before the snow starts to melt!

HANDWRITING

Lucy's psychiatry booth is very popular and sometimes there's a long queue of people waiting for advice. Lucy writes down the number of people she sees each time she's open. A number on its own can also be called a digit.

1 Copy these digits 5 times.

1

2

3

4

5

6

7

8

9

2 Now write each number as a word.

one

two

three

four

five

six

seven

eight

nine

SUFFIXES

Linus is very smart and often surprises his friends with the long words he knows. Did you know you can make words longer by adding certain letters to the end? A group of letters added to the end of a word is called a suffix.

A suffix is a letter, or group of letters, that can be added to the **end** of root words. A root word is the main part of a word.

1 -**ing** turns words into verbs – doing words.

see + **ing** = seeing

Turn these words into verbs, by adding the suffix -**ing**.

a. break + ing = _____

b. hunt + ing = _____

c. build + ing = _____

d. buzz + ing = _____

e. jump + ing = _____

f. cook + ing = _____

2 For these words, adding -**er** means **more**. We can add -**er** to compare.

bright + **er** = brighter
My torch is bright**er** than the candle.

Make these words mean more, by adding the suffix -**er**.

a. fast + er = _____

b. light + er = _____

c. short + er = _____

d. long + er = _____

e. cold + er = _____

3 The suffix -**ed** can be used to say a verb that has already been done.

paint + **ed** = painted
The door has been paint**ed** red.

Turn these verbs into the past tense by adding the suffix -**ed**.

a. listen + ed = _____

b. work + ed = _____

c. farm + ed = _____

d. hunt + ed = _____

e. cook + ed = _____

SPELLING PRACTICE

Charlie knows that the best way to learn how to spell words is to practise lots. He's come up with some fun ways for you to practise spelling common words.

Making up a rhyme or acrostic poem can help us to remember how to spell tricky words.

Here are a few ideas for tricky spellings:

Laugh

Laugh
And
U
Get
Happy

Because

Big
Elephants
Can
Always
Understand
Small
Elephants

Can you make up an acrostic to remember how to spell beautiful? The first few ideas have been added for you.

Big
Ears
Are
Useful
T _____
I _____
F _____
U _____
L _____

1

Write your own acrostic to help remember the spelling of these words.

People

P _____
E _____
O _____
P _____
L _____
E _____

Friend

F _____
R _____
I _____
E _____
N _____
D _____

2

Sometimes, it helps to look for smaller words within words.

there also has the word **here** in it — can you see it? **T**here

Look at these words. Underline the smaller word in each one. The first one has been done for you.

a. t<u>here</u>   **b.** another   **c.** improve   **d.** gold   **e.** across   **f.** children

PREFIX un-

Peppermint Patty is happy when she's playing baseball and unhappy when she's doing homework. The prefix **un-** means not, so is often used to mean the opposite.

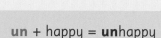

un + happy = **un**happy

1

Lucy is jealous of Charlie's glowing school report so she's added the prefix **un-** to make some of the words mean the opposite! Remove the **un-** prefix to make the report positive again.

a. Charlie is very unfriendly. _____

b. Charlie always keeps his desk untidy. _____

c. Charlie is unaware of the school rules. _____

d. Charlie is unpleasant to have in the class. _____

2

Add the prefix **un-** to the words below but be careful, there are two words that can't use it! Cross these words out.

___ happy   ___ lucky   ___ eat   ___ well   ___ believable

___ do ___ sleep   ___ even   ___ kind   ___ pack

Say the word out loud to help you decide if the prefix can be added.

3

Decide whether each word needs the prefix **un-** to make the meaning match the picture. If it needs **un-**, write it in front of the word. The first one has been done for you.

a. The rock is **un**comfortable.

d. Linus is being ___ helpful.

b. Woodstock is ___ dressed.

e. Charlie is feeling ___ happy.

c. Sally is ___ interested.

f. Lucy is being ___ kind.

ADJECTIVES

Charlie and Linus are playing a 'guess who?' game using adjectives to describe people. Do you want to join in the fun?

Adjectives describe nouns. They can go before or after nouns in a sentence. Using a variety of adjectives to add description is one way to improve writing.

Snoopy has a **red kennel**.

Adjective   Noun

1

Draw lines to join each adjective to the picture it describes.

yellow	smelly	relaxed
tired	sad	excited
happy	friendly	cold

2

Underline the adjective (a word that describes a person, place or thing) in each of these sentences.

a. The cosy nest is Woodstock's home.

b. Sally ate a delicious cupcake.

c. It was a sunny day.

d. Charlie flew a colourful kite.

e. Peppermint Patty found an old baseball.

f. Linus is a loyal friend.

oo SOUNDS

It's Halloween so everyone is practising their spooky **oo** sounds! Did you know there are different ways of spelling that sound? Say your best scary **oo**!

1 The words below have the same **oo** sounds but are spelt differently. Help the Peanuts gang to remember these spellings by writing them in the correct box.

| new | rude | mood | tube | huge | flew | blue | blew | cool | use |
| clue | spoon | few | pool | moon | grew | lagoon | tune | | |

oo	ue	ew	u-e

Can you think of any more words with the long **oo** sound?

2 Choose a word from the box above to fill the gap in each sentence.

 a. Lucy is in the p ___ l.

 d. Ice-cream keeps you c ___ l.

 b. Snoopy is looking for a cl ___.

 e. Snoopy's coat is h ___ g ___.

 c. Charlie is playing a t ___ n ___.

 f. The present is bl ___ .

SUFFIXES

Charlie Brown's baseball team is playing a game. The game is happening now so the words to describe it have to be in the present tense.

Verbs that are happening now usually have the suffix **-ing**. The suffix **-ed** changes a word into the past tense for things that have finished.

I am watch**ing** the game. – I watch**ed** the game.

Can you see how the word endings change the meaning of the word? Sometimes the suffix makes the spelling change:

Double the last letter	**Remove the silent** e
stop – stop**p**ing – stop**p**ed	dance – dancing – danced
slip – slip**p**ing – slip**p**ed	announce – announcing – announced
drop – drop**p**ing – drop**p**ed	hope – hoping – hoped

1 Add the **-ing** suffix to these words. Remember to double the last letter.

a. jog _____ **b.** run _____

c. win _____ **d.** hop _____

e. tap _____ **f.** swim _____

2 Add the **-ed** suffix to these words. Remember to double the last letter.

a. nap _____ **b.** beg _____

c. hug _____ **d.** top _____

e. rub _____ **f.** grab _____

3 Complete these sentences. You need to choose the suffix **-ed** or **-ing**. Remember to double the last letter.

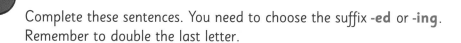

a. Charlie is (run) _____ to catch the ball.

b. Linus has (play) _____ on Charlie's team for a long time.

c. Schroeder isn't very good at (catch) _____ the ball.

d. Sally is (watch) _____ her big brother play.

e. Lucy has (miss) _____ the ball again.

HANDWRITING

Sally is planning her birthday party. She wants the invitations to look perfect so she's practising her handwriting before she writes them. Can you help her by practising your handwriting too?

1 This group of letters start at the top, go straight down, then back up again.

b h k m n p r

Can you write each letter 5 times? Start at the top, go straight down, then back up your line.

b   n

h   p

k   r

m

2 Copy each of these words three times. Don't forget to leave a finger space between your words.

pink _____   rim _____

hip _____   prim _____

DAYS OF THE WEEK

It's the school holidays and Sally has had a busy week. She's kept a diary to remember all the things she's done.

1

Help Sally write her diary by putting the days of the week in the right order. The first one has been done for you.

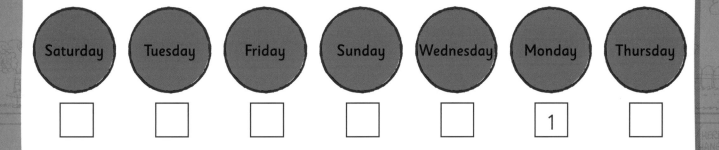

Saturday	Tuesday	Friday	Sunday	Wednesday	Monday	Thursday
☐	☐	☐	☐	☐	1	☐

2

Can you add the correct letters to Sally's diary so that the days are spelt correctly?

M ____ day: I watched TV in my beanbag chair.

Tu ____ day: Linus, my sweet babboo, came to call for Charlie.

W ____ esday: I watched Charlie's baseball game.

Th ____ sday: Lucy taught me how to use a skipping rope.

Fr ____ ay: I made a hobby horse out of a mop and a paper bag.

Sa ____ day: I spotted Charlie at Lucy's psychiatrist booth.

Su ____ y: Snoopy found my diary! Now I need a new hiding place.

Top Tip
The names for the days of the week are proper nouns, so they have a capital letter.

3

Check the spellings as you write the answers to these questions.

a. Which day did Sally make a hobby horse?

_____

b. Which day comes before Friday?

_____

c. Which day did Sally watch TV?

_____

d. Which two days make the weekend?

_____

19

EXPANDED NOUN PHRASES

See page 15 to find out more about adjectives.

Schroeder has brought his piano in for show and tell. He's using adjectives to describe his love of classical music to the rest of the class.

Adjectives describe nouns. Here are some examples of adjectives.

amusing	brave	clean	jolly	quiet	quick	sweet	spooky	juicy	gloomy
delicious	tiring	busy	active	fun	dark	colourful	untidy	slimy	wooden

1

Underline the adjectives in these sentences. There might be more than one!

a. Schroeder's piano is red.

b. Playing the piano is a fun, rewarding hobby.

c. After a long, tiring day, Snoopy relaxes by listening to Schroeder's music.

d. Schroeder is a happy, thoughtful friend.

Did you know?
An expanded noun phrase is a phrase that has at least one adjective describing the noun. If using two adjectives together, they should be separated by a comma.

2

Remember to put a comma between two adjectives.

These simple noun phrases do not have any adjectives. Can you turn each one into an expanded noun phrase by adding one or two adjectives? You can choose adjectives from the box at the top of this page or think of your own.

The ball – the **colourful, bouncing** ball

a. The piano - _____

b. The t-shirt - _____

c. The house - _____

d. The town - _____

CONJUNCTIONS

Charlie enjoys writing book reports but wants to get better at it. Help give him some feedback on his latest report by completing the questions below.

Conjunctions are words that can join two short sentences together. **And**, **but** and **so** are conjunctions (joining words) that are used to connect parts of a sentence that are related.

Charlie stayed up late writing his report **so** he is very tired.

1

Can you join the two pieces of text together using the conjunction that fits best? The first one has been done for you.

a.

Charlie's writing is messy

His report isn't long enough

and
but
so

it is hard to read.

he has lost marks.

b.

Charlie used long sentences

He needs to improve his spelling

and
but
so

descriptive words.

grammar.

c.

Charlie tries hard

His ending is good

and
but
so

sometimes he overthinks things.

he has repeated the last sentence.

Remember capital letters and full stops.

2

Write a sentence of your own for each conjunction.

_____ but _____

_____ and _____

_____ so _____

SYLLABLES

Sally's class is practising a song for a school concert. To help her sing in time to the music, Sally needs to understand about syllables in words.

Syllables are the different parts or beats in a word. Each syllable will always have a vowel sound.

Sal – ly	syl - la - ble
= 2 beats	= 3 beats
so 2 syllables	so 3 syllables

1

Clap for each beat as you say these words.

Snoopy = Snoo - py = 2 claps

Typewriter = type - wri - ter = 3 claps

Charlie = Char - lie = 2 claps

Kite = kite = 1 clap

2

Sort the words from Sally's song into the correct number of syllables so that she can sing it in time to the music.

| fun   wish   happy   tomorrow   sing   unbreakable |
| together   lonely   forever   memories   share   never |

1 syllable	2 syllables	3 syllables	4 syllables

POETRY

Miss Othmar is teaching the class about poetry. She likes poems that rhyme. Rhyming words end with the same sound, even if they are spelt differently.

| meet | street | neat | petite |

1

Say these words out loud, then group the words that rhyme together by drawing a ring around each group.

play   trees   sky   begun   dry

high   cry   friend   end

sun   bees   day

2

Join in the lesson by choosing words that rhyme from the words above.

The sun was shining in the sky,

Birds were flying way up _____ .

The wind was whistling through the trees,

The flowers were filled with bumble _____ .

But then a dark cloud covered the sun,

Before long, rainfall had _____ .

The playing children gave a cry,

And quickly ran off home to _____ .

3

Read the poem below. Can you spot the pairs of rhyming words at the end of each line? When you see them, underline them.

He manages the baseball team,
To win a game is his big dream.

Reading comic books is what he
likes to do,
And he'll always share with you.

Even when things don't go right,
He doesn't quit, he puts up a fight.

Do you know who I'm talking about?
It's Charlie Brown, without a doubt.

PUNCTUATION

Charlie Brown is reading a book about how to fly a kite but Snoopy has walked all over it and the punctuation marks are covered in muddy pawprints! Oops!

Punctuation are symbols that help make sentences clearer.

Full stop	**Comma**	**Exclamation mark**	**Question mark**
.	,	!	?
At the end of every sentence.	To separate items in a list and between two parts of a sentence (clauses).	At the end of a sentence that is angry, shouted or needs to make a point.	Instead of a full stop at the end of a question.

1 Can you put the full stops and capital letters back so that Charlie can read the first page of the book?

f you want to learn how to fly a kite, you will need a lot of patience

his book will teach you everything you need to know

2 Charlie wants to read chapter 1. Can you add the missing punctuation marks so that the text makes sense?

Are you ready to begin To fly a kite successfully, you will need a dry day

an open space a strong wind and lots of practice Follow the instructions

in this book and soon your kite will be flying high

COMPREHENSION

Snoopy is a Beagle Scout Master. His troop has just come back from a hike. Read all about it below, then answer the questions.

1

Read this and have a go at answering the questions. You may need to read it more than once.

The Beagle Scouts set off on their hike at first light. They had everything they needed, including pizza, a surfboard and a sundial. They headed into the woods but the wind blowing through the trees scared Olivier, a squirrel frightened Bill, and Fred jumped when a branch touched his head. They stopped for lunch so everyone could calm down but after eating all the pizza and cake, they were too full to move. A rest was in order. Unfortunately, they fell asleep. By the time they woke up, it was getting dark so they headed home. Needless to say, nobody gained a Beagle Scout Award.

a. When did the Beagle Scouts set off on their hike? _____

b. Where did they go? _____

c. What frightened Olivier? _____

d. Why did Fred jump? _____

e. What did the troop eat for lunch? _____

f. Do you think the hike was successful? _____

_____

2

Draw a picture of the Beagle Scouts on their hike in the woods.

SUFFIXES FOR NOUNS

Today at school, Charlie and his classmates are learning how to add a suffix to a word. Miss Othmar won't mind if you join in the lesson too!

If I **ride** the bike, I am the **rider.**

When adding suffixes **-er** and **-ness**, sometimes the spellings need to change. These spelling rules will help:

-er

If the root word ends with a single consonant after a single vowel, double the consonant.

swim + **er** = swimmer

If the root word ends in **e**, drop the **e** before adding **er**.

ride + **er** = rider

-ness

If the root word ends in **y**, change **y** to **i**.

happ**y** = happiness

1

Add **-er** to turn the verb into the noun - the person who does that action. Look for clues for when to change the spelling.

a. speak _____

d. swim _____

b. jog _____

e. play _____

c. sing _____

f. teach _____

2

Turn these adjectives (describing words) into nouns by adding **-ness**. Look for the clue for when to change the spelling.

a. thick _____

d. still _____

b. well _____

e. happy _____

c. ill _____

f. sad _____

HANDWRITING

When Snoopy is writing with his typewriter, he always remembers to use a capital letter at the start of every sentence and for proper nouns.

Capital letters are taller than lower case letters.

1

Practise writing each of the letters below as a capital and in lower case. Can you make a character's name using some of the letters?

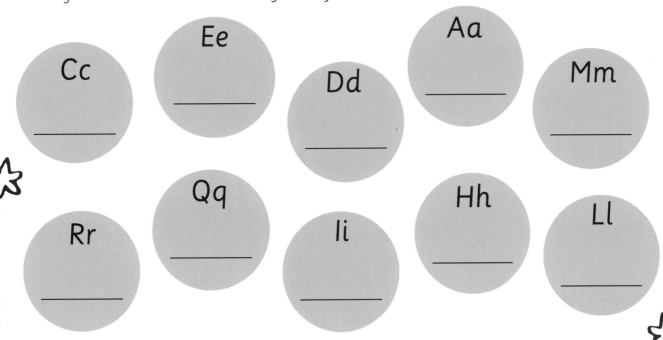

Ee

Cc

Aa

Dd

Mm

Qq

Hh

Rr

Ii

Ll

The character's name is _____

2

Put the missing capital letters into these sentences.

a. _____noopy likes to write stories.

b. _____e has a very good imagination.

c. _____aybe one day he will publish a book.

d. _____harlie Brown would definitely buy it!

HOMOPHONES

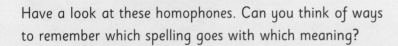

I see the sea! Have you noticed how some words sound the same, but mean different things? They're called homophones.

Homo = same   **phone** = sound

Have a look at these homophones. Can you think of ways to remember which spelling goes with which meaning?

hear/here	won/one	mail/male	night/knight
sea/see	sun/son	pear/pair	whole/hole

1

Put the correct homophones into the gaps.

Listen to that! Can you h_____ it? It's the sound of the s_____ as the waves crash

against the shore. It's a lovely day h_____ at the beach. The s_____ is shining and the

waves are big. Can you s_____ Peppermint Patty surfing on the waves? She is very good

and has even w_____ a surfing competition! Charlie Brown isn't as good but he's trying! He's

spent the w_____ day learning how to surf and he won't get home until n_____ time.

2

Here are some more homophones. Choose which spelling makes sense for each sentence.

there - a place	**their** - belongs to them	**they're** - short for they are
Oh, **there** you are.	It is **their** kite.	**They're** very late today.

a. What are you doing over _____? Come over here.

b. Who has dropped _____ drawing on the floor?

c. Charlie Brown and Snoopy are good friends. _____ going to the park together.

d. At school, Charlie and his classmates are handing in _____ book reports.

28

PAST, PRESENT AND FUTURE

SCAN CODE

purple mash

Snoopy is imagining another fantasy life. This time, he's travelled in a time machine and is stuck in the future! Help bring him back to the present by completing the activities below.

The spelling of verbs can give us clues to the tense, whether the action happened in the past or present.

The verb ending **ing** can indicate present tense and **ed** can indicate past tense.

Words before the verb also give us clues to the tense.

was, **were** = show the past tense

is, **are**, **am** = are used in the present tense

will, **shall**, **going to** = show the verb will happen in the future

1

Circle whether each sentence is about the past, present or future.

a. Snoopy belongs to Charlie Brown.   Past   Present   Future

b. Snoopy ate pancakes for breakfast.   Past   Present   Future

c. Snoopy has a good imagination.   Past   Present   Future

d. Yesterday, Snoopy imagined he was a WW1 pilot.   Past   Present   Future

e. Snoopy is going to the library tomorrow.   Past   Present   Future

f. Snoopy was tired after his time travelling adventure.   Past   Present   Future

2

We know that some verbs add **ed** to turn them into the past tense, but other verbs change completely. Draw lines to match each irregular verb with the past tense verb. The first one has been done for you.

I eat pizza.	I caught the ball.
I see it.	I swam in the sea.
I run across the field.	I ate pizza.
I swim in the sea.	I wrote in my diary.
I write in my diary.	I ran across the field.
I fall over.	I saw it.
I catch the ball.	I fell over.

SUFFIX -tion

Miss Othmar is fed up with finding bubble gum stuck under the school desks! She's given the class a science project to invent something to get rid of the gum. When you invent something, it's called an invention.

The suffix -tion (sounds like 'shun') can turn verbs into nouns.

Charlie is working on his inven**tion**.

If the word ends in **t** add **ion**

If the word ends in **te** get rid of the **e** and add **ion**

1

Change these words to end in -tion.

a. invent - _____

b. create - _____

c. act - _____

2

Choose the best -tion word for these sentences.

| invention | vacation | creation | addition | action | station | celebration | solution |

a. The classmates must find a s_____ to solve the gum problem.

b. Marcie is very happy with her gum removal i_____.

c. Charlie is planning a c_____ for Snoopy's birthday.

d. Sally is looking forward to her summer v_____.

e. Snoopy likes to be at the centre of the a_____.

f. To catch the train, you must go to the train s_____.

3

Use **Look**, **Say**, **Cover**, **Write**, **Check** to practise these spellings.

creation _____

celebration _____

addition _____

action _____

30

HANDWRITING

Sally loves letters with curves because they remind her of one of her favourite foods – spaghetti! Practise writing Sally's favourite letters below.

Let's warm up! Stretch out your fingers then curl them up. Now wiggle them as quickly as you can.

1 Write each letter slowly and carefully 3 times.

c a d e g o q f s b

c

a

d

e

g

o

q

f

s

b

STORYTIME

This story is all about Charlie and the kite-eating tree. Can you read it aloud?

1

One day, Charlie Brown woke up feeling excited. Today was the day he was finally going to beat the kite-eating tree! He dressed quickly and grabbed his kite from the cupboard.

Charlie walked to the park and stood at the top of a hill. He took a deep breath and started to run. The kite bumped along the ground, then it flew up into the air. Charlie couldn't believe his eyes. Now all he had to do was stay away from the kite-eating tree.

Suddenly, Charlie heard a yell from behind him. He turned to see a small child on a bike wobbling towards him. Before he could move out of the way, the child crashed into him and I think you can guess what happened next. That's right, Charlie accidentally let go of the kite string, then the kite flew away and was gobbled up by the kite-eating tree. Better luck next time, Charlie Brown.

Can you put these things that happened in the story in the correct order? The first one has been done for you.

☐	Charlie's kite was eaten by the kite-eating tree.
1	Charlie woke up feeling excited.
☐	A child on a bike crashed into Charlie.
☐	Charlie walked to the park.

2

Can you write two more sentences to add to the story?

_____

_____

POSSESSIVE APOSTROPHE

The Peanuts gang are playing their musical instruments – loudly! Complete the activity below to show which instrument belongs to which friend.

An apostrophe with an s - **'s** - is used to show something belongs to a particular person.

Lucy**'s** flute – the flute belongs to Lucy.

1

Write the owner's name next to each instrument. Put the **'s** after their name to show it belongs to them. The first one has been done for you.

Charlie	Snoopy	Lucy	Schroeder	Linus

a. Snoopy's _____ saxophone.   **b.** _____ piano.   **c.** _____ accordion.

d. _____ trombone.   **e.** _____ trumpet.   **f.** _____ guitar.

COMPREHENSION

Charlie Brown has seen an advert in the comic book store window for a new comic book. He's saving up his pocket money so that he can buy it.

Coming Soon!

Calling all comic book fans! Get ready for the most exciting launch of all time! This brand-new, action-packed comic will hit the shops on Monday.

Bursting with adventure, it includes:
- Classic characters
- New characters
- Exclusive stories
- Unseen artwork
- Bonus pages
- Free posters

Pre-order inside to get your copy before it sells out!

1

Answer these questions about the text:

a. Circle the style of writing that best fits the text above.

Poem   Narrative/story   Advert

b. What is this text trying to persuade you to do?

_____

c. When will the comic book be in the shops?

_____

d. Find two words (adjectives) to describe the comic.

_____

e. What free content will come with the comic?

_____

f. Why might someone want to pre-order the comic?

_____

g. Would you buy the comic book? Why or why not?

_____

HANDWRITING

Lucy is practising her handwriting so that she can write a really neat love letter to Schroeder! You can practise yours below.

Let's warm up! Do a little dance with your arms and fingers to get them moving. Squeeze your shoulders up to your ears and then relax them back down again. When your fingers are warmed up, make sure you are holding your pencil properly and sitting tall at your table.

1 Each of these letters has a zig zag shape. Write each letter slowly and carefully 3 times.

V   X   W   Z

V

W

X

Z

2 Copy these words carefully. You can look back at the previous handwriting pages to see how to write the other letters.

van _____

win _____

mix _____

zip _____

Practise the words until your letters are even sizes.

SPELLING SEARCH

Peppermint Patty loves sports. Can you find some of her favourite ones hidden in this wordsearch?

1

Find the words in this wordsearch. Look across, down and diagonally. Tick off the words as you find them.

- ☐ hockey
- ☐ swimming
- ☐ skating
- ☐ tennis
- ☐ surfing
- ☐ football
- ☐ baseball
- ☐ golf
- ☐ basketball
- ☐ volleyball

v	o	l	l	e	y	b	a	l	l
s	k	a	t	i	n	g	a	l	s
d	r	w	t	e	k	l	a	s	g
t	e	n	n	i	s	b	o	l	o
a	w	f	o	o	t	b	a	l	l
s	e	r	t	e	k	g	h	m	f
h	o	c	k	e	y	v	c	x	n
i	o	s	w	i	m	m	i	n	g
p	a	f	s	u	r	f	i	n	g
b	a	s	e	b	a	l	l	d	w

SUBORDINATE CLAUSES

Linus has volunteered to help Miss Othmar rewrite the school rules – he'll do anything to spend more time with his favourite teacher! Can you help too?

When, **if**, **that** and **because** are conjunctions (joining words) used to add extra information (a subordinate clause) to the main part of a sentence (the main clause). The main clause can form a complete sentence on its own. A sentence that has a subordinate clause is called a complex sentence.

> I like playing baseball **because** it keeps me fit.

Main clause
Makes sense on its own.

Subordinate clause
Adds extra information to the main clause.

1

Use each conjunction once to complete these sentences.

when	that	if	because

a. Do not run in the corridor _____ **it is dangerous.**

b. Go straight to class _____ **the bell rings.**

c. Put your hand up _____ **you have a question.**

d. There are two parts to show and tell _____ **must be completed to get a reward sticker.**

2

Here are some more sentences with conjunctions. Draw a line to join the two parts of each sentence.

a. Marcie wears glasses   when he visits Lucy's psychiatry booth.

b. Charlie must pay 5 cents   because it is comfortable.

c. Snoopy sleeps on top of a kennel   if you need help.

d. Put your hand up   that is red.

e. Sally loves her beanbag chair   when he plays baseball.

f. Charlie wears a mitt   because they help her see better.

SUFFIXES -er and -est

Peppermint Patty is practising hockey and the noise is disturbing Lucy, who's trying to read. Lucy is using adjectives like 'louder' and 'noisiest' to complain about Peppermint Patty!

If the adjective ends in two consonant letters (the same or different), the ending is simply added on. small = small**er**	If the root word ends with a single consonant after a single vowel, double the consonant. sa**d** = sa**dd**er	If the root word ends in **e**, drop the **e** before adding **-er**. ride = rid**er**	If the root word ends in **y**, change **y** to **i**. happ**y** = happ**i**est

1

These adjectives can be made even stronger by adding the suffixes **-er** or **-est**. Draw lines to join the adjectives that have a matching root word. The first one has been done for you.

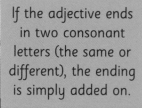

noisy   happier   noisiest
happy   lazier   laziest
lazy   louder   loudest
loud   noisier   happiest

> **Did you know?**
> **-er** is used to compare adjectives. Charlie is fast**er** than Linus at running.
> **-est** is used to make a superlative adjective, meaning the most. Charlie is the fast**est** runner.

2

Now that Peppermint Patty has stopped practising hockey, Lucy is being much kinder to her and has used some different words to describe her. Can you add the suffix **-er** or **-est** to each one? The first one has been done for you.

a. kind ___kinder___ ___kindest___

b. sad _____ _____ (watch out for a spelling change!)

c. tall _____ _____

d. bright _____ _____

e. busy _____ _____ (watch out for a spelling change!)

f. lonely _____ _____ (watch out for a spelling change!)

PROGRESSIVE TENSE

School has finished until tomorrow. Can you complete the sentences below using the past, present and future tense?

Progressive verbs show an action continues to happen; it is an ongoing action. This can be in the past, present, or future. The words before the verb tell us the tense of the ongoing action.

Past	Present	Future
was **+** -ing were I **was** walking	are is **+** -ing am I **am** walking	will be **+** -ing shall be I **will be** walking

1

Choose **was** or **were** to make the sentences correct for the **past** tense.

a. Linus and Pig Pen _____ late for school.

b. Miss Othmar _____ in a good mood today.

2

Choose **are**, **is** or **am** to make the sentences correct for the **present** tense.

a. I _____ going to do my homework.

b. Marcie _____ helping Peppermint Patty with her maths.

3

Add **will be** to make the sentences correct for the **future** tense.

a. Linus _____ _____ doing show and tell tomorrow.

b. I _____ _____ playing baseball after school.

SUFFIXES CROSSWORD

Marcie has finished her schoolwork before everyone else so Miss Othmar has given her a crossword to do. Can you complete it too?

1

Choose the correct suffix to add to the root word to solve the clues.

-ment   -ness   -ful   -less   -ly

The suffixes **-ment**, **-ness**, **-ful**, **-less** and **-ly** start with a consonant letter, so can be added to most root words without changing the spelling.

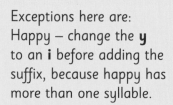

Exceptions here are:
Happy – change the **y** to an **i** before adding the suffix, because happy has more than one syllable.

Play – keeps the **y** because the word play has only one syllable.

CLUES

Across

5. Be _____ when you throw the ball. (care)

6. Charlie Brown's team is quite _____ at baseball. (hope)

7. Miss Othmar enjoys her _____ at the school. (employ)

Down

1. Charlie was filled with _____ when his kite was eaten by the kite-eating tree. (sad)

2. You can see the _____ on Schroeder's face when he plays the piano. (enjoy)

3. Charlie's baseball team lost the game because they played _____. (bad)

4. Snoopy is a very _____ character. (play)

HANDWRITING

You've practised all the letter shapes with the handwriting activities in this book. Now it's time to put them together.

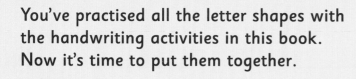

water   bear
find   these

1

Copy these sentences. Try to keep your letters even and smooth.

a. I like being dirty!

b. I am a dust magnet!

c. Don't make me have a bath!

d. Dirt is my friend!

e. Being different is good.

ADVERBS

Sally has written a play and wants Charlie to be the main character! He's not so sure but has agreed to practise the part. Sally is using adverbs to explain how he should act.

An adverb gives more information about the verb. Adverbs show how, when or where the verb is happening. Many adverbs are created by adding the suffix **-ly** to the end of an adjective.

careful + ly = careful**ly**

Charlie is speaking **loudly**

↑   ↑   ↑

noun   verb   **adverb**

1

Here are some of the words Sally has used to direct Charlie. Can you circle the adverbs? Watch out, there are some verbs in there too!

shout	carefully	walk	excitedly
quietly	cheerfully	play	suddenly

Remember
If a word ends in **y**, change the **y** to an **i** before adding **-ly**.
happy = happ**ily**

2

Add **-ly** to the word in brackets to create an adverb that adds detail to each sentence.

a. Woodstock is flying _____ (excited)

b. Franklin is going to bed _____ (sleepy)

c. Sally is eating cupcakes _____ (greedy)

d. Lucy is sleeping _____ (peaceful)

e. Peppermint Patty is dancing _____ (crazy)

f. Snoopy is playing the trumpet _____ (loud)

3

Make up your own sentences for this picture, adding an adverb.

_____

_____

CONTRACTIONS

Marcie always calls Peppermint Patty 'Sir'! Peppermint Patty has decided that Marcie speaks too formally so she's trying to help her sound chattier!

Contractions join two different words together to make one shorter word. These words need an apostrophe.

I'll (instead of I will) The **apostrophe** shows that letters have been missed out.	I'm (instead of I am) The **apostrophe** shows a letter has been missed out.

1

Match the contractions to the full words.

she'll	should not
shouldn't	would not
I've	he had
he'd	she will
wouldn't	I have
who's	who is

2

Write these contractions in full. The first one has been done for you.

a. haven't = <u>have not</u>

b. couldn't = _____

c. I'm = _____

d. we'll = _____

3

Now you know how to contract words, write what Marcie should change these phrases to so that she sounds less formal.

a. did not = _____

b. they will = _____

c. I will = _____

d. there is = _____

COMPREHENSION

Something exciting has happened overnight and Charlie and his friends are in for a surprise! Read the text to find out why, then answer the questions below.

1

One morning, Charlie Brown was woken up by his little sister, Sally, bursting into his room to tell him it was snowing and school was closed for the day. Hurray!

All of Charlie's friends gathered outside to play ice hockey on the frozen pond. But when Charlie came out of his house, he was carrying his kite instead of his skates. Only Charlie Brown would try and fly a kite in the snow!

Charlie took hold of his kite string and ran through the snow. The kite lifted off the ground and floated into the air. But suddenly, Charlie tripped and got tangled up in the kite string. A gust of wind blew the kite and Charlie was dragged onto the pond, right into the middle of the ice hockey game!

Snoopy gasped as the puck slid across the ice towards Charlie. Charlie kicked the puck out of the way and watched in amazement as it flew into the net. Charlie had scored the winning goal!

a. Why was Sally excited?

_____

b. What game did the friends want to play on the frozen pond?

_____

c. What was Charlie carrying when he came out of the house?

_____

d. How did Charlie end up on the frozen pond?

_____

e. Which verb (action word) is used to tell the reader what Charlie did to the puck?

_____

f. How do you think Charlie felt after scoring the winning goal?

_____

_____

NON-FICTION COMPRENSION

Did you know that Snoopy is a beagle? Read on to find out lots more about this friendly breed of dog, then answer the questions about the text.

Beagles were originally bred for hunting. Lots of beagles have white tips on their tails – this was bred into beagles so that they would be easier to spot when they had their noses to the ground during a hunt.

Beagles are noisy dogs! They are one of the most vocal breeds and can make three different sounds – a bark, a yodel-like sound called a bay, which they use when they're hunting, and a howl.

Beagles are tiny when they are born, weighing less than 0.5kg. They grow up to be friendly, easy-going and very playful. Sociable beagles enjoy being around people and other dogs, which is why they're popular pets.

Beagles have a great sense of smell. A beagle's long ears help them to sniff out smells as they catch scent particles and keep them close to the dog's nose. This allows them to take in as much information about the scent as possible.

1 Are these sentences true or false? Find the answers in the text above.

a. Beagles are friendly dogs.   TRUE ☐ FALSE ☐

b. Lots of beagles have a black tip on their tail.   TRUE ☐ FALSE ☐

c. Beagles can make four different sounds.   TRUE ☐ FALSE ☐

d. Beagles use their ears to help them smell.   TRUE ☐ FALSE ☐

ANSWERS

Page 2: Nouns

1. **person:** boy, friend, sister
   place: pond, room, library, town, teacher
   animal: squirrel, rabbit
   thing: chair, plane, cookie, bike

2. Lucy, Sally, Tuesday

Page 3: Finger spaces

1. a. 5 words
   b. 6 words
   c. 6 words

2. a. Baseball ⓥ is ⓥ a ⓥ great ⓥ sport.
   b. Players ⓥ must ⓥ work ⓥ as ⓥ a ⓥ team.
   c. Teams ⓥ should ⓥ practise ⓥ lots ⓥ to ⓥ improve.

3. Learn how to win at baseball

Page 5: Sentence builder

1. a. Pig Pen is walking.
   b. Snoopy is driving.
   c. Charlie is falling.
   d. Linus is smiling.

2. a. The library is busy.
   b. It is a hot day.
   c. Charlie is talking.

Page 6: ee sounds

1.

ee	ea	ie
see	sea	field
tree	dream	thief
green	tea	shriek
meet	each	chief
keep	neat	
teeth	clean	

2. a. teeth   b. sea   c. green
   d. tree   e. neat   f. field

Page 7: Comprehension

1. a. false   b. true   c. false
   d. true   e. false

Page 8: Plurals

1. a. snails   b. doors   c. eggs
   d. homes   e. brushes   f. churches
   g. foxes   h. lunches

2. a. burgers   b. wishes   c. balls
   d. kisses   e. beaches   f. dishes

Page 9: Verbs

1. f. There are lots of possible answers. Examples include: run, jump, clap, dance, laugh, shout, sit and hop.

2. a. skating
   b. waiting
   c. ate
   d. playing

3. There are lots of possible answers. Examples include:
   a. reading, thinking, drawing and sleeping
   b. daydreams, eats, laughs and barks
   c. playing, skating, writing and resting

Page 10: Story sequencing

1. 1. Roll a large ball of snow for the body.
   2. Roll a smaller ball of snow for the head.
   3. Place the head on top of the body.
   4. Decorate the snowperson.

2. First, they drag the box to the top of the hill.

   Then, they sit in the box.

   Next, they push off from the top of the hill.

   Finally, they slide down the hill.

Page 12: Suffixes

1. a. breaking   b. hunting
   c. building   d. buzzing
   e. jumping   f. cooking

2. a. faster   b. lighter
   c. shorter   d. longer
   e. colder

3. a. listened   b. worked
   c. farmed   d. hunted
   e. cooked

Page 13: Spelling practice

1. Acrostic ideas are children's own choice. Encourage your child to use words that will help them to remember the spellings.

2. a. there   b. another
   c. improve   d. gold
   e. across   f. children

Page 14: Prefix un-

1. a. friendly   b. tidy
   c. aware   d. pleasant

2. The two words that can't use the prefix un- are eat and sleep.

3. a. uncomfortable   b. dressed
   c. uninterested   d. unhelpful
   e. unhappy   f. unkind

Page 15: Adjectives

1.

relaxed   cold   excited

friendly   smelly   yellow

sad   happy   tired

2. a. cosy   b. delicious
   c. sunny   d. colourful
   e. old   f. loyal

Page 16: oo sounds

1.

oo	ue	ew	u-e
mood	blue	new	rude
cool	clue	flew	tube
spoon		blew	huge
pool		few	use
moon		grew	tune
lagoon			

2. a. pool   b. clue   c. tune
   d. cool   e. huge   f. blue

Page 17: Suffixes

1. a. jogging   b. running
   c. winning   d. hopping
   e. tapping   f. swimming
2. a. napped   b. begged
   c. hugged   d. topped
   e. rubbed   f. grabbed
3. a. running   b. played
   c. catching   d. watching
   e. missed

Page 19: Days of the week

1. Monday, Tuesday, Wednesday, Thursday, Friday, Saturday, Sunday.
2. M<u>on</u>day
   Tu<u>es</u>day
   W<u>edn</u>esday
   Th<u>ur</u>sday
   Fri<u>d</u>ay
   Sa<u>tur</u>day
   S<u>un</u>day
3. a. Friday
   b. Thursday
   c. Monday
   d. Saturday and Sunday

Page 20: Expanded noun phrases

1. a. red
   b. fun, rewarding
   c. long, tiring
   d. happy, thoughtful
2. There are many correct answers. Examples include:
   a. The small, red piano.
   b. The soft, stripy t-shirt.
   c. The big, old house.
   d. The noisy, busy town.

Page 21: Conjunctions

1. a. so   b. and   c. but
2. Read your child's sentences together to check that they make sense.

Page 22: Syllables

2.
1 syllable	2 Syllables
fun	happy
wish	lonely
sing	never
share	

3 syllables	4 syllables
tomorrow	unbreakable
together	
forever	
memories	

Page 23: Poetry

1. play and day
   high and sky
   trees and bees
   sun and begun
   cry and dry
   friend and end
2. high, bees, begun, dry
3. team and dream, do and you, right and fight, about and doubt

Page 24: Punctuation

1. If you want to learn how to fly a kite, you will need a lot of patience. This book will teach you everything you need to know.
2. Are you ready to begin? To fly a kite successfully you will need a dry day, an open space, a strong wind and lots of practice. Follow the instructions in this book and soon your kite will be flying high.

Page 25: Comprehension

1. a. At first light.
   b. The woods.
   c. The wind blowing through the trees.
   d. A branch touched his head.
   e. Pizza and cake.
   f. There are many correct answers here as long as your child can give a reason for their answer. Examples include: no because they didn't hike very far, no because lots of the Beagle Scouts were scared, and no because nobody gained a Beagle Scout Award.

Page 26: Suffixes for nouns

1. a. speaker   b. jogger
   c. singer   d. swimmer
   e. player   f. teacher
2. a. thickness   b. wellness
   c. illness   d. stillness
   e. happiness   f. sadness

Page 27: Handwriting

1. Charlie
2. a. Snoopy
   b. He
   c. Maybe
   d. Charlie

Page 28: Homophones

1. hear, sea, here, sun, see, won, whole, night
2. a. there   b. their
   c. they're   d. their

Page 29: Past, present and future

1. a. Present   b. Past
   c. Present   d. Past
   e. Future   f. Past
2. I eat pizza. → I ate pizza.
   I see it. → I saw it.
   I run across the field. → I ran across the field.
   I swim in the sea. → I swam in the sea.
   I write in my diary. → I wrote in my diary.
   I fall over. → I fell over.
   I catch the ball. → I caught the ball.

Page 30: Suffix -tion

1. a. invention   b. creation
   c. action
2. a. solution   b. invention
   c. celebration   d. vacation
   e. action   f. station

Page 32: Storytime

1. 1. Charlie woke up feeling excited.
   2. Charlie walked to the park.
   3. A child on a bike crashed into Charlie.
   4. Charlie's kite was eaten by the kite-eating tree.
2. Read your child's sentences together to check that they make sense.

Page 33: Possessive Apostrophe

1. a. Snoopy's saxophone.
   b. Schroeder's piano.
   c. Linus's accordion.
   d. Lucy's trombone.
   e. Snoopy's trumpet.
   f. Charlie's guitar.

Page 34: Comprehension

1. a. Advert.
   b. The advert is trying to persuade you to buy a new comic book.
   c. Monday.
   d. Brand-new and action-packed
   e. Posters.
   f. To get a copy before it sells out.
   g. All answers are correct!
      Encourage your child to give reasons why they have given their answer.

Page 36: Spelling search

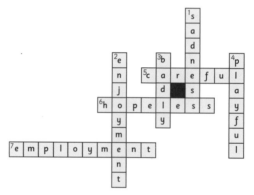

Page 37: Subordinate clauses

1. a. because
   b. when
   c. if
   d. that
2. a. Marcie wears glasses because they help her see better.
   b. Charlie must pay 5 cents when he visits Lucy's psychiatry booth.
   c. Snoopy sleeps on top of a kennel that is red.
   d. Put your hand up if you need help.
   e. Sally loves her beanbag chair because it is comfortable.
   f. Charlie wears a mitt when he plays baseball.

Page 38: Suffixes -er and -est

1. noisy, noisier, noisiest
   happy, happier, happiest
   lazy, lazier, laziest
   loud, louder, loudest
2. a. kinder, kindest
   b. sadder, saddest (double the consonant before adding the suffix)
   c. taller, tallest
   d. brighter, brightest
   e. busier, busiest (y changes to i before adding the suffix)
   f. lonelier, loneliest (y changes to i before adding the suffix)

Page 39: Progressive tense

1. a. were   b. was
2. a. am   b. is
3. a. will be   b. will be

Page 40: Suffixes crossword

Page 42: Adverbs

1. carefully, excitedly, quietly
   cheerfully, suddenly
2. a. excitedly
   b. sleepily
   c. greedily
   d. peacefully
   e. crazily
   f. loudly
3. There are lots of different correct answers. One idea might be: Charlie and Snoopy are dancing excitedly.

Page 43: Contractions

1. she'll — she will
   shouldn't — should not
   I've — I have
   he'd — he had
   wouldn't — would not
   who's — who is
2. a. have not   b. could not
   c. I am   d. we will
3. a. didn't   b. they'll
   c. I'll   d. there's

Page 44: Comprehension

1. a. It was a snow day.
   b. ice hockey
   c. a kite
   d. He was tangled up in the kite string and a gust of wind blew the kite and dragged him onto the pond.
   e. kicked
   f. There are many correct answers here as long as your child can give a reason for their answer. Examples include: surprised because he wasn't even playing ice hockey, amazed because he's not usually very good at sports, happy because he helped win the game, disappointed because although he scored a goal in ice hockey, he still didn't manage to fly the kite.

Page 45: Non-fiction comprehension

1. a. true
   b. false
   c. false
   d. true